LIFE IS TOO SHORT TO HAVE BORING HAIR

A Real-Life Coloring Book for Hairdressers

by J Erskine

Published by
Arf! Arf! Studios

LIFE IS TOO SHORT TO HAVE BORING HAIR
A Real-Life Coloring Book for Hairdressers
by J Erskine

Published by
Arf! Arf! Studios
Canmer, KY

arfarfstudios.com

Life is too short to have boring hair

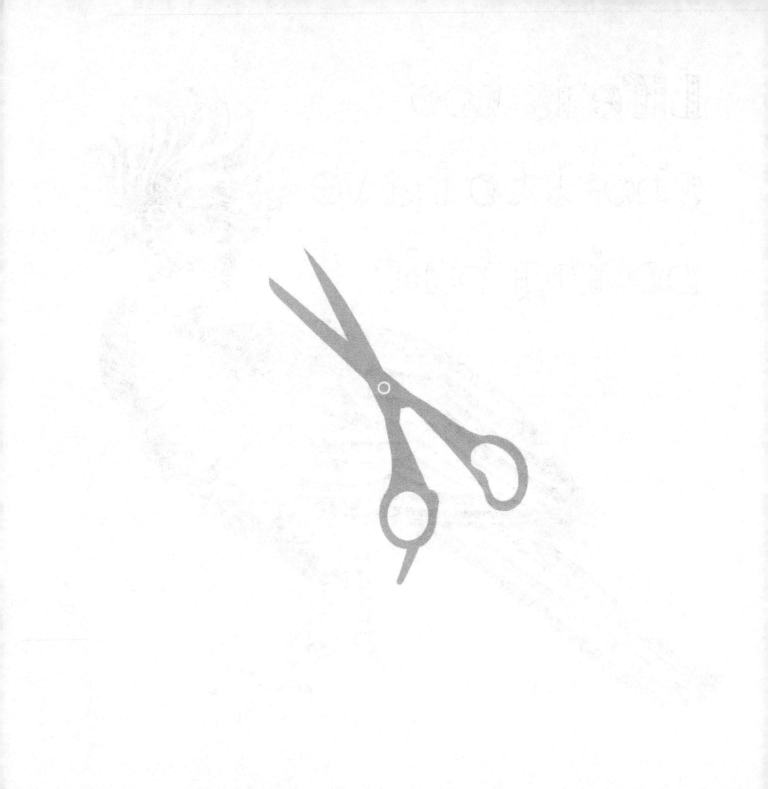

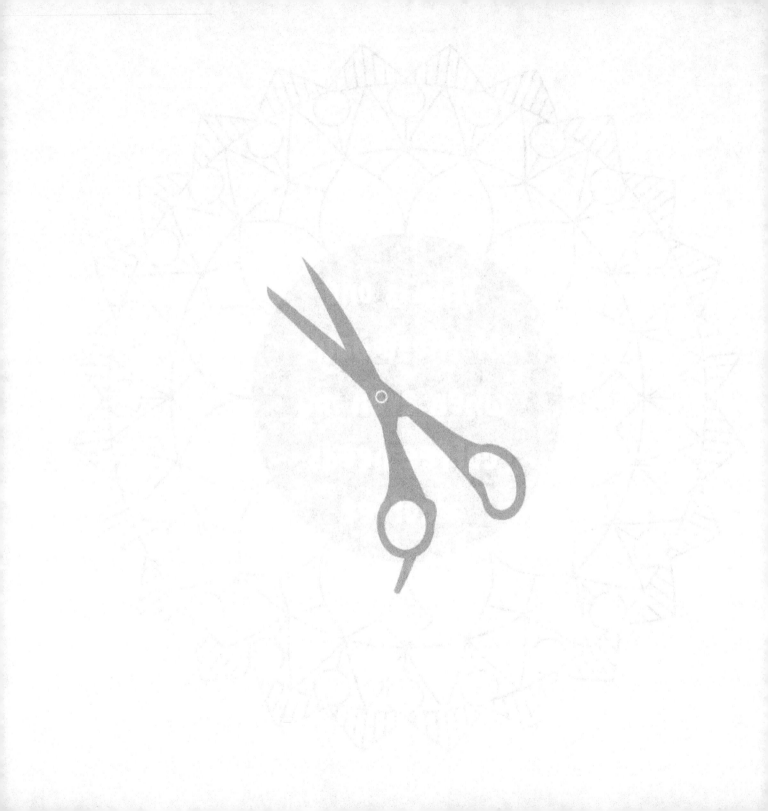

"I TAKE MY HAIR STYLIST'S ADVICE
A LOT MORE SERIOUSLY
THAN I DO MY SHRINK'S"

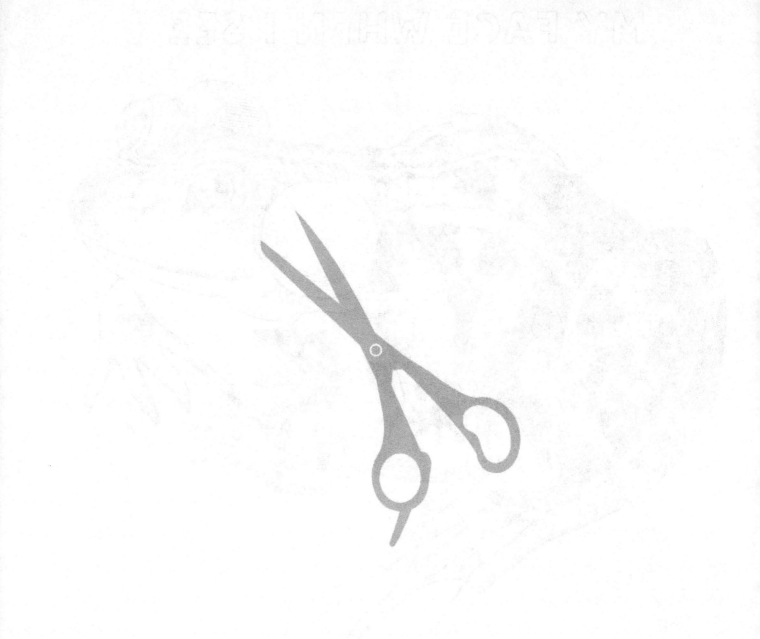

INNER BEAUTY IS AWESOME

BUT A LITTLE HAIRSPRAY NEVER HURTS

You can't control everything. Your hair is meant to remind you of that.

OMG,
a customer almost
DIED
in front of me today.

But then I counted
to ten and put the
scissors back
in the drawer.

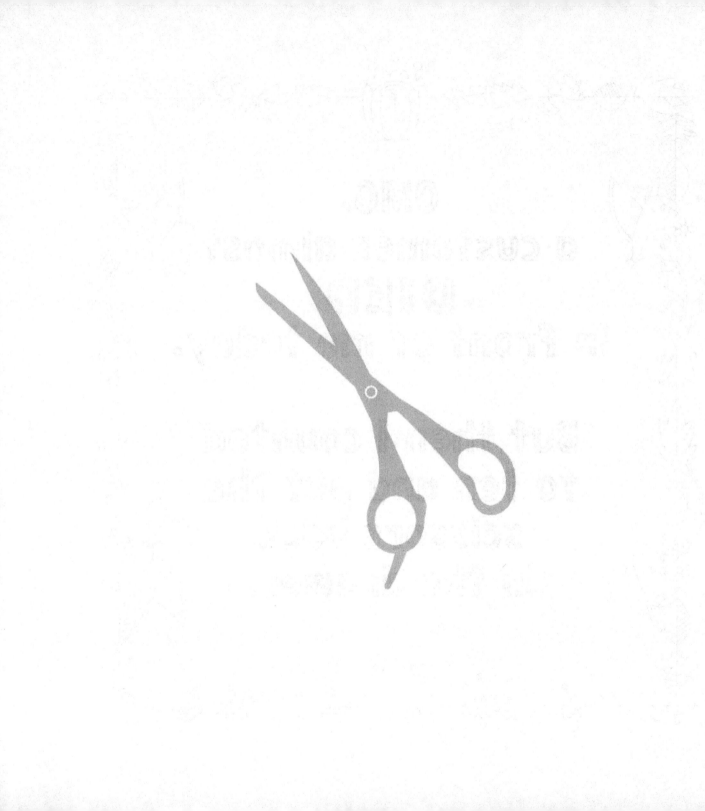

ALL OF LIFE'S PROBLEMS
CAN BE SOLVED

WITH A FABULOUS HAIRCUT

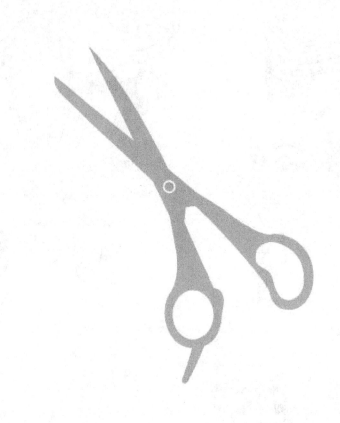

HONEY,
IF YOU THINK
WHAT I SAY
OUT LOUD
IS AWFUL,
YOU SHOULD
HEAR ME
WHEN I
KEEP TO
MYSELF.

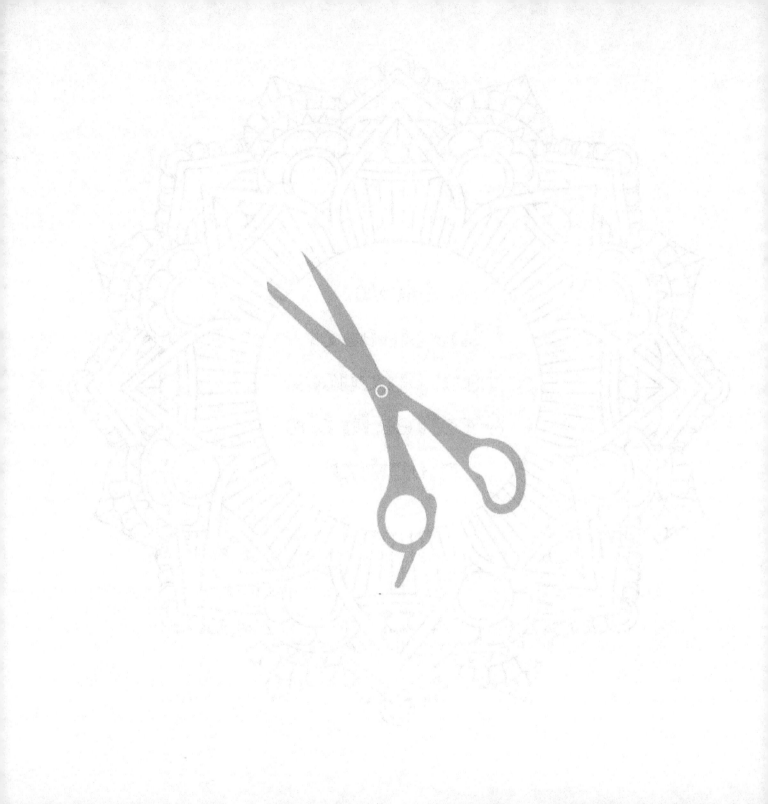

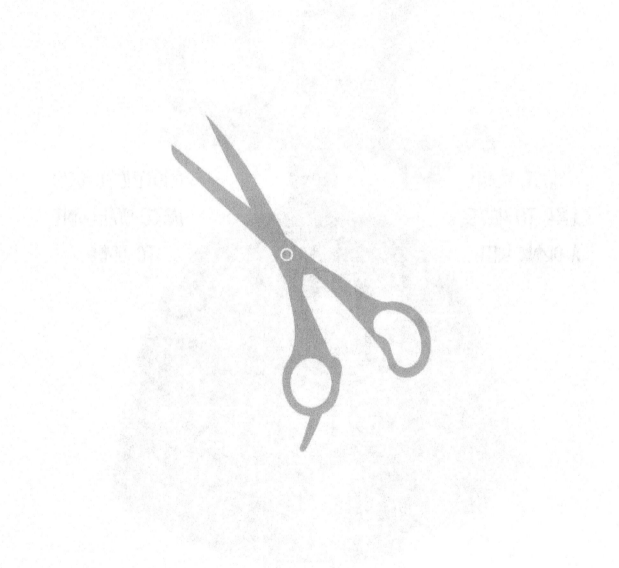

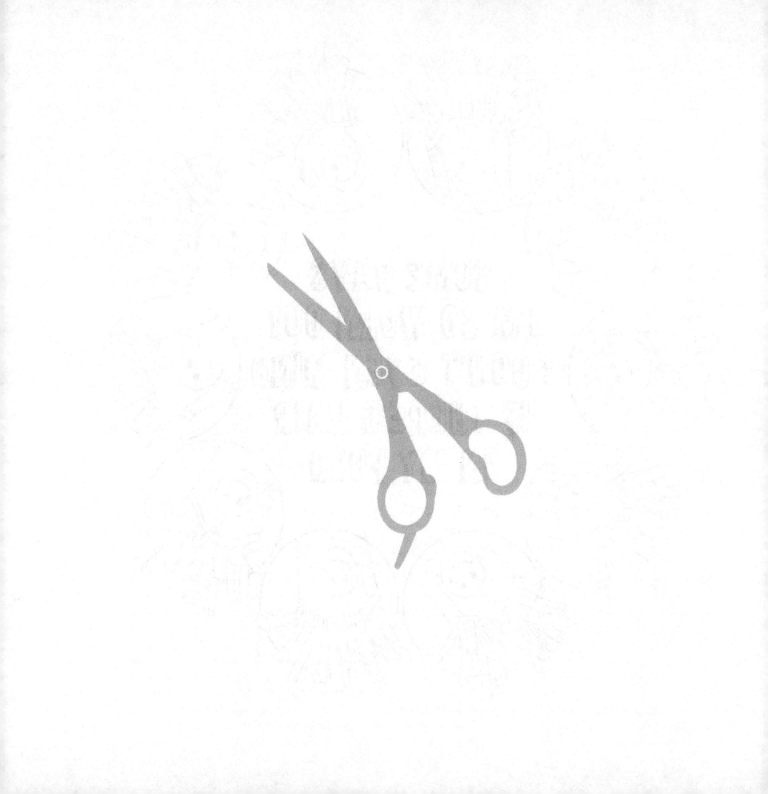

GREY HAIR IS
JUST GOD'S WAY
OF KEEPING
US IN BUSINESS

IF MONDAY WAS
A HAIRCUT,
IT WOULD BE
A MULLET.

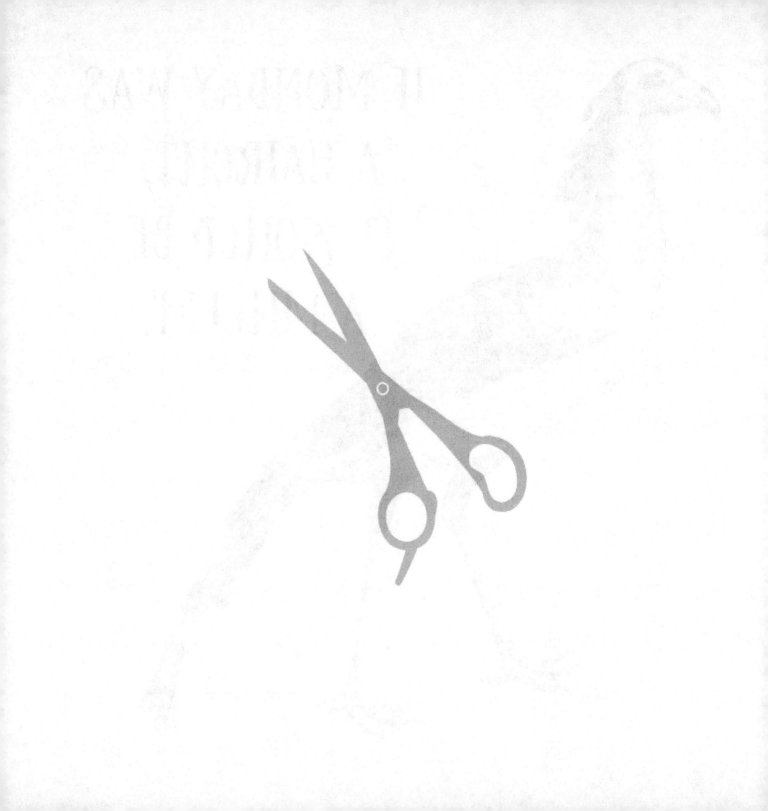

HAIRSTYLING WOULD BE A GREAT CAREER IF YOU JUST DIDN'T HAVE TO DEAL WITH PEOPLE

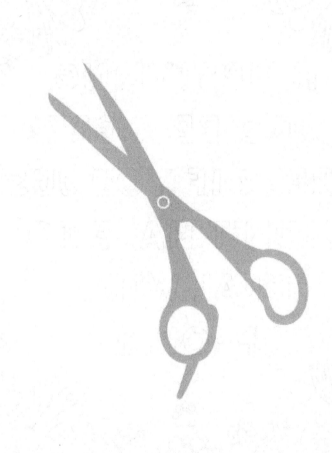

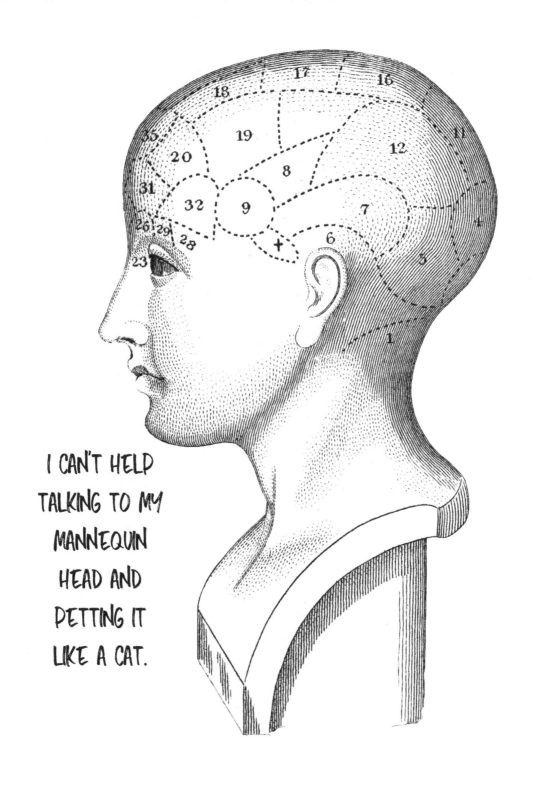

I CAN'T HELP
TALKING TO MY
MANNEQUIN
HEAD AND
PETTING IT
LIKE A CAT.

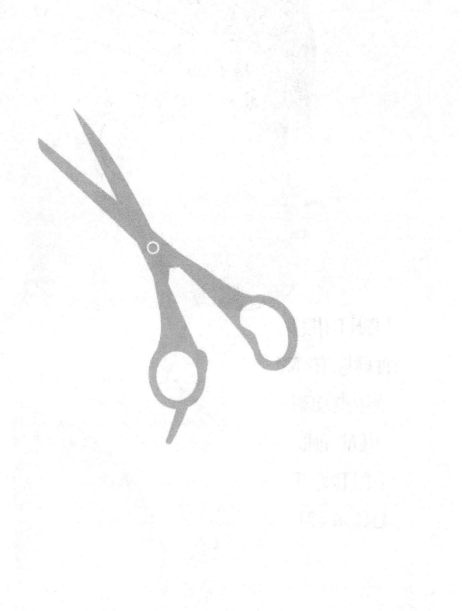

SOMETIMES
I JUST HAVE
TO TELL MYSELF

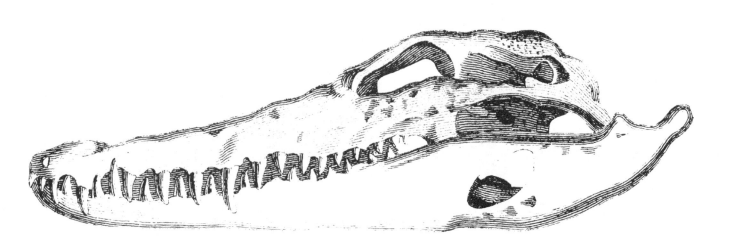

IT'S NOT WORTH
THE JAIL TIME

LIFE IS FULL OF CHALLENGES
AND FRUSTRATIONS... BUT
EVENTUALLY YOU FIND A
HAIR STYLIST YOU LIKE

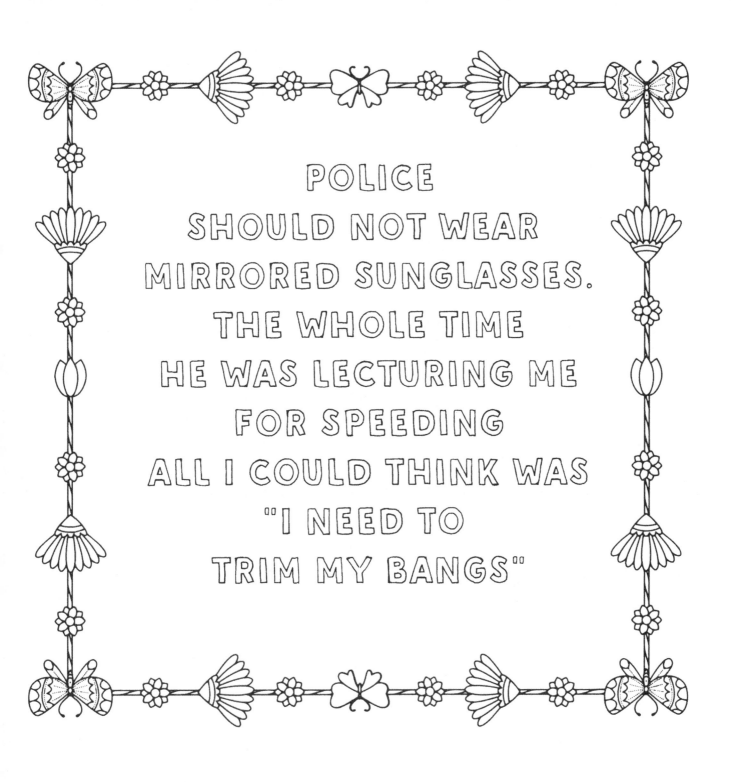

POLICE
SHOULD NOT WEAR
MIRRORED SUNGLASSES.
THE WHOLE TIME
HE WAS LECTURING ME
FOR SPEEDING
ALL I COULD THINK WAS
"I NEED TO
TRIM MY BANGS"

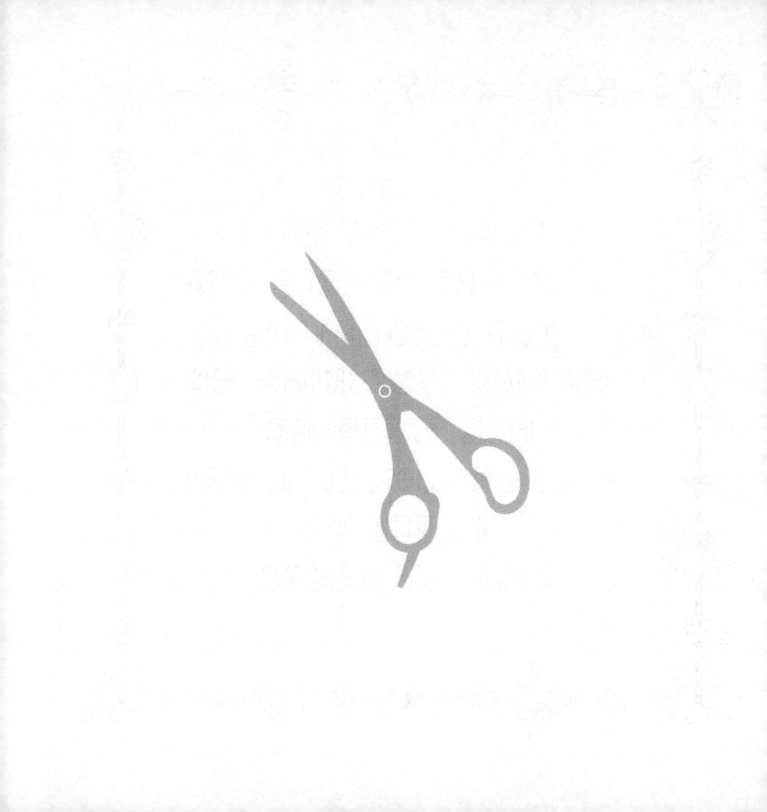

If we can't
make you look good

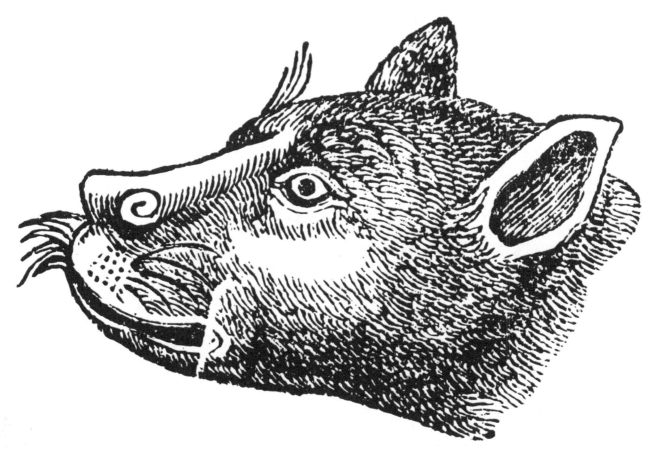

you ugly

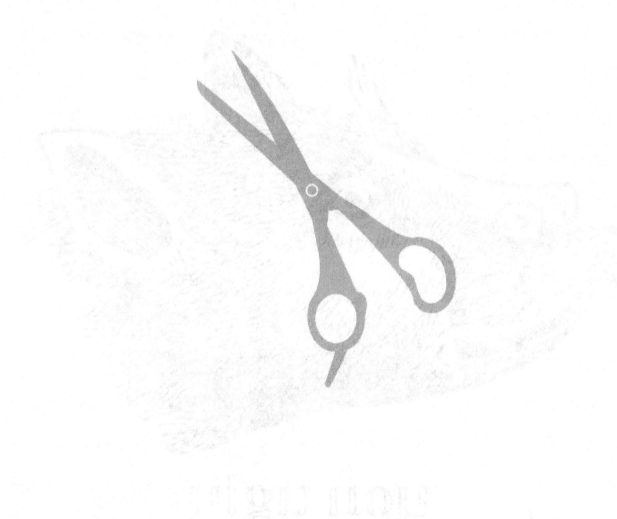

IT'S FINE IF YOU'RE UNDRESSING ME WITH YOUR EYES, JUST DO NOT MESS UP MY HAIR.

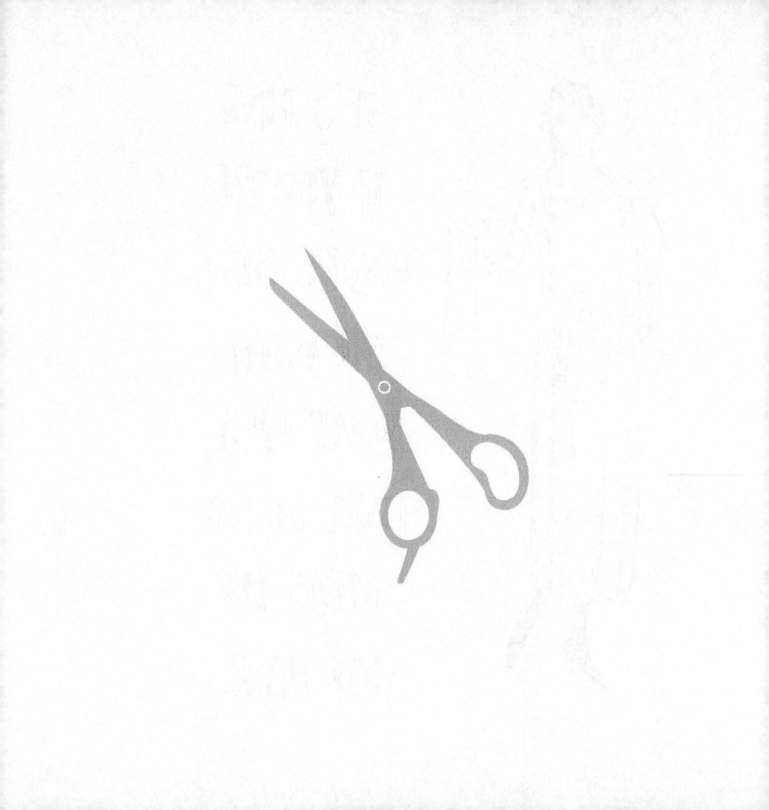

I just hate wasting
a good hair day
when there's no one
important to see me

I MAKE HAIR CONTACT

LONG BEFORE I MAKE EYE CONTACT

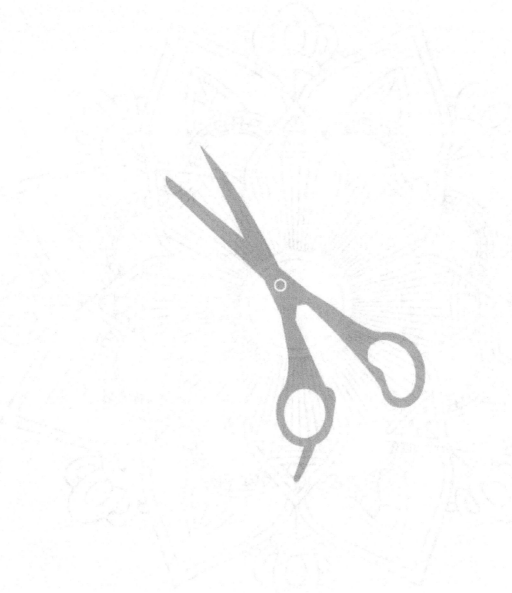

BEAUTY COMES
FROM THE INSIDE.

INSIDE THE
HAIR SALON.

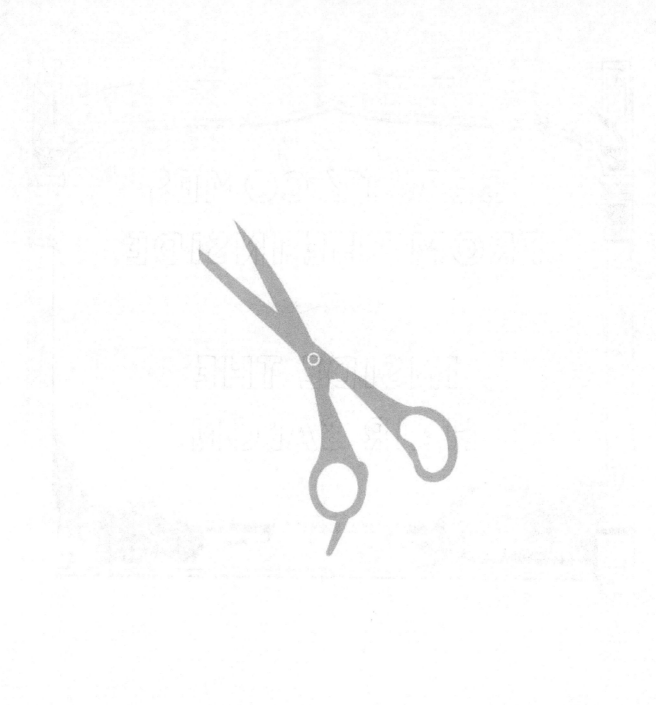

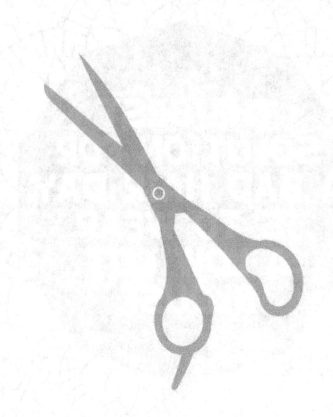

SHHH... SHHH... SHHH...

NOBODY CARES.

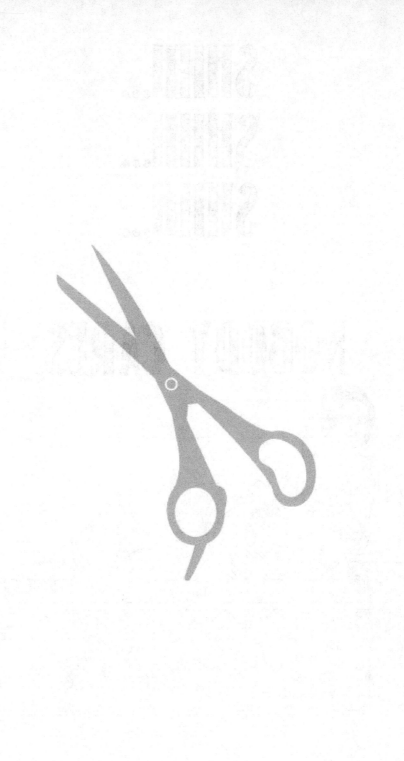

A Word to the Wise:

Never piss off your hair stylist.
Ever.

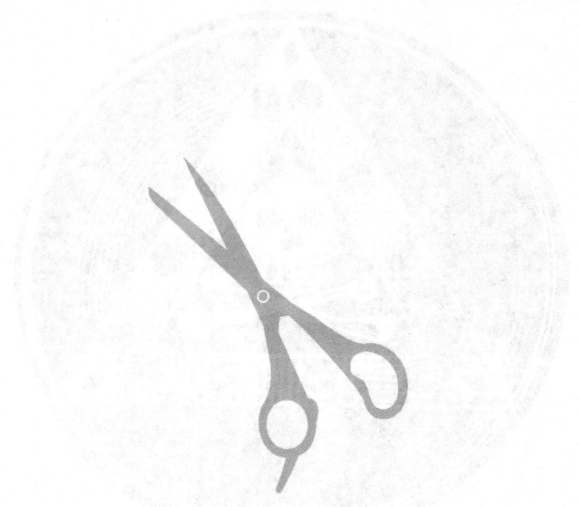

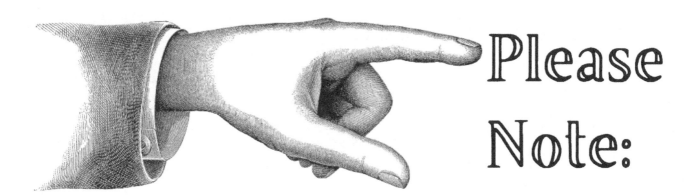

Please Note:

Hair service prices are totally subject to change according to customer's attitude.

TRULY,
BLESSED ART
THE HAIRDRESSERS,

FOR THEY BRING OUT
THE BEAUTY
IN OTHERS.

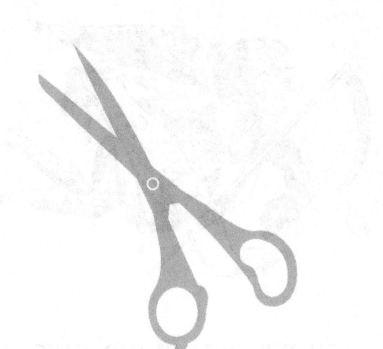

Made in the USA
Las Vegas, NV
06 September 2023

77138229R00044